After the Ritual

After the Ritual

Tom Henihan

Ekstasis  Editions

Library and Archives Canada Cataloguing in Publication

Henihan, Tom
    After the ritual / Tom Henihan.

Poems.
ISBN 1-894800-89-3
ISBN 978-1-894800-89-1

    I. Title.

PS8565.E5824A64 2006   C811'.54   C2006-905460-6

© 2006 Tom Henihan
Front cover art and design: Boyd Chubbs

Acknowledgements:
The author would like to thank The Newfoundland and Labrador Arts
Council for its support in completing this manuscript.

Published in 2006 by:
Ekstasis Editions Canada Ltd.   Ekstasis Editions
Box 8474, Main Postal Outlet   Box 571
Victoria, B.C. V8W 3S1   Banff, Alberta T0L 0C0

Printed in Canada

Ekstasis Editions wishes to thank the following for their support of its pub-
lishing program: the Canada Council for the Arts, and the Province of British
Columbia through the British Columbia Arts Council.

For Paddy

Contents

Moving to an Island

He leaned against the deck rail of the late evening ferry watching an oily rainbow float on the darkening water. Beyond the mantle of the harbour lights and the dirty cup of his sleeplessness, voices working and bantering reached him, foreign as someone else's comfort. The soft evening rain gave him solace, but the smell of creosote and salt emanating from the waves, paced him for an endless voyage.

As the ferry pulled away he felt this passage to the island as a kind of severe verdict on his life but the vigour of being on the ocean again allowed him to embrace his predicament in a consummate manner. He lit a cigarette and leaned again on the deck rail: all the days he had lived were out there between the darkening sky and the water and everything he wanted had accumulated into a vague and persistent yearning, which was also tied to the gestures of the sea.

He loved the sea and the rain and grottoes of white metallic light draped with storm clouds. The sea always spoke to him directly, in its placid moments and in its turbulence and excess. The sea exercised a pull on his spirit with its wild relentless surface and its serene and mysterious depths.

He also loved boats, no matter how humble or ostentatious: he saw something heroic in the bow of a ship, curved like a musical instrument, rising and dipping in the waves. Boats were beautiful and brave, yet there was something gentle and shrine-like about their shape and affirmative colours.

He rubbed the deck rail with his hand, feeling the smooth contours of the paint applied over the rough corroded steal. He recognised an element of joy in the depth of his conundrum and enjoyed the lure of the ocean as it drew him out under the sky. Though he had lived on the margin for so long, he now felt that he had given himself too much shelter. Greater physical contact with the world would have given his life more substance and provided the metaphors he needed to construct its meaning.

A blast of the ship's horn roused him as the ferry sailed through a narrow pass. On the small islands he passed the last traces of a dusky blue light hung above the trees and gently dissipated into grey gauze above the water. The soft muted light of late evening made the prim houses above the bays appear like miniatures. He admired the sense of order the houses evoked but their orchestrated comfort suggested a repose that was too conclusive.

Seeing the other passengers loitering about with a pleasant air of adjournment, he felt isolated and restless. He looked out over the water, asked himself why he was travelling to the island and realized, as on so many other occasions, that he was moving just for the sake of moving. A sense of futility quickly rose within him and he could feel his eyes burn and fill with the greyness of the sky.

He found the obsession to move harrowing but unrelenting. He didn't travel, he just drifted. He was one of those people with too much of one thing in the blood: too much fervour, too much anger, too much bitterness, too much remorse; too highly pitched on one frequency ever to attend to life properly. Occasionally he felt peacefully alone: other times, he found himself pacing desperately at the threshold, hoping for a way to be reinstated. The impulse to move had cost him everything. His only fraternity were the misbegotten ones driven by a vehement impulse coded in the blood like a distant star: the ones with a perpetual sense of loss and the distance of the world in their eyes, eyes burning with the weary desperation of maverick planets.

He wished he could stay out on the water forever, moving through the darkness and shards of broken light, with the excited dogs of the waves leaping at the sides of the ship. But the lights of the island's ferry dock slowly rose out of the water like an effusion of things he could recognize in the firmament. The words *distance* and *loss* came to his lips and sat like two stone dogs in front of his heart. Around the harbour lights, the darkness seemed to accumulate with unforgiving authority. Distance and loss: if only those dogs would bark or bite but they seemed to recognize the dark night as their master.

Spirit of Place

The vital pigments of that landscape
are always with me
and detonate occasionally in potent dreams.
There the spirits of the dead seem happy.
There the horses are also pure spirits,
they are messengers returning from the other side
(the message being that they have returned)
and they appear at ease and indifferent
to the gifts that they bring,
to the energy of heaven leaving tracks in the snow.

Strange how I came to that place late
and now it has taken up residence within me—
it holds what is essential to me
and returns things that are lost,
like love that has died,
in moments of longing I could never give up.

I love the most distant of its distant perimeters
that touch the sky
and that draw like the moon on water
on the viscose substance
of my most stubborn wounds.
I want no other house but this.

I need the long tongues of silence
that run like ravines through the heart of that world.
I need the sparks of blue snow
and wires of light in its northern sky.
I need the stillness of the air that rattles
and the subtle waves of music that breathe
like new foals in the flames of the yellow grass.

Things We Have Abandoned

The things we have abandoned shame us,
because we embraced them once
or because we abandoned them.

So many obsolete colours unfurl in the breeze,
the belief they dressed has died, leaving the cold moon,
the swaying grass and the hills in the distance.

Other than love and hate, we go on playing
small roles in other peoples lives,
looking out from the hermetic shack of our own bones

at clouds that accumulate and disappear,
revealing a sweeping yellow light
and storms that consume themselves like sulphur.

Castle Mountain

The stone cup of this green country fills up with memories,
the prospect renders the evening large
and demands from us that we praise its emptiness.

The blue air perfumed with resin hangs close to the trees.
The shallow river is a wolf of iron and light heading out across the stones.

But we didn't come here just for this:
we are here for the things we lost and the things we are longing for
and we are here also to bid farewell to the victories we have put aside.

Time owns our hearts, the proud stones that touch the sky,
the relentless river, and the grass that grows in the crevices.

Indifferent to nothing for a moment we feel stranded,
but you smile and I am taken
by the small shrine of your mouth and the gentle waterfall of your laughter.

An Evening Ceremony

An arena for devotion has been cleared
under the dying hands of the sky, the sleeping canyons dream in red,
their diaphanous breath a paragon of patience and death.

The temperament of the leaves is gentle with acceptance.
The smooth conscience of the river, meeting a cataract of monumental stone,
achieves the pure and childlike prayers of falling water.

People and animals trample the clay,
and the rising dust that aspires to dress the wounded hands of the sky
anoints the gentle contours of the world.

Leave-taking

Just as we were learning to live
death kissed her cheek
and a new frontier appeared in her eyes.
All clouds became attached to her burial.
Her nervous hands became leaves
dallying with their shadows.
When she tried to play
there was a hint of the casket in the wine.
At night, her arid pain seared the dark room.
All day long, just like the ocean and the sky
moving relentlessly in their caves,
the prow of her sadness
rose and dipped in strange waves.

Road Map

She considers the chart of her own hand,
a white space,
a northern map with few settlements.

Touched by its emptiness
her spirit swells like an ocean in its cage.
She wishes she had taken time to travel.

She patrols with the fingers of her other hand,
the tiny blue rivers
and the narrow roads wrenched from the distance.

She thinks of the bridal whiteness
of the luminous snow
and the exotic spice of silence from the north.

She is astonished by her life, by gifts left unopened,
by the fact that she has lived so far from this.
Astonished that she never tried to play her hand.

Resolute Silence

It is raining with a resolute silence,
the mountains with their heads thrown back
wash their noble profiles.

I miss you and feel foreign once again,
here in this place I had learned to call home.

But how important is all this … this missing you
in a world that remains as vague and fleeting
as rain falling on a mountain lake.

Although

Although we are so small when we die
our passing is as large as the sun going down
and as forlorn as a fire's weary tongue
diminished against the breast of the cold night.

Our fingers woven in prayer,
we depart in a cloud that rises from our bones
and all the secrets we planned to unleash on the world
like horses, just drift away in a turbulence of snow.

The Limits of the World

The sun, travelling long distances between Sabbaths,
marks the sky with its bleeding feet.
The wind in the grass whispers and reminisces,
but there is nothing absent here
except what I need to feed my necessary yearning.
Serious as a child re-enacting some crucial ritual,
the moon appears from the limits of the world.
Flanked by one another against the sky,
horses graze leisurely,
while the mountains in the distance,
staunch and detached as executioners,
draw on their hoods of religious darkness.
In the brooding cradle of the river valley
the predatory night thickens its coat in the moist air.

Roots

If you ask me where I live
I will point to the threshold between sleep and death.
Awake I just wander these streets cold as the inside of a camera
pursued by my shadow of dark rainwater.

Women, remote in the atmosphere of their perfume,
fight off the world with pinions of sharp light
that emanate from the eyes of their bracelets.
Men beat their tin cups looking for praise and love,
but the day keeps all its doves captive.

A church spire, against a sky darkened like heated paper,
recognizes the void as God
and promises that behind the tedium of still water
the freedom of fever endures.

Because the legends from desolate places still instruct me,
I head for the neighbourhoods that never wake
from their thin and disturbing sleep.
The roots that probe my daydreams with dirty fingers
drink from beneath the bridges that I cross.

Down here, poverty bathes in a vapour of gasoline
and the tide debauches itself before reaching the sand.
The people's flesh is pale with the dust of an arduous past
but there is something in their eyes that's imminent.
The smoke that travels towards the sky is theirs.
Hungry for order for a moment I close my eyes.

I make my way back along the soft edges of the water
where the tall exotic grass brandishes its jagged blades.
The rusted sheets of iron are skins the sun and rain have shed
and the bandaged knees of children are small companion planets.

As the evening deepens
the city rises like a crystal that has been forbidden to cry.
Arriving back, a tired illusion of myself waits for me at every corner.
All I want is to be detached from my own weariness.

When the canyons of the sky are no longer paved with sulphur
and the gentle twilight, compassionate with the odour
of wine and coffee, withers over the water,
I accept my mission like the waves,
drink from the cool water of the moon and head home.

Our Endless Petition

In a universe too large to ever feel complete,
even in sleep we maintain our constant petition.

And though we may reject being nurtured
on the rough stones of old beliefs
and tutored on the curved instrument of the sky,
we still must guard our certainty
against the same prevailing winds.

How long can we ignore
the things we whisper to ourselves,
and how long can we withhold the fact
that we need the energy of obligation
to climb each hill.

Outside of faith,
like animals caged outside language,
we are cut from the full length of the light,
from the glowing shrine
to the pilgrim's bleeding feet.

Broken Nails

A large window presides
over the cold postponement of the white sky
and the hard seconds that drop to the floor
like broken nails.

The devout stillness of the birds beneath the eves,
their colours soaked in iron,
is a vigil to waiting for a change in the wind
for a new direction through the transient light.

It is physical, the effort of the soul to find comfort
and the strength to carry the heart's aptitude for loneliness.
The world out there possesses the stately depth
and smooth detachment of an old mirror.

Cross of Light and Water

Why did I return, to be greeted only by the rain.
Is this my home, this kingdom crowned with thorns
kept barbarous by that rain.

When you pierce this world it bleeds
the excrement of livestock
and reveals the stones of martyrdom.

It is a cross fashioned from light and water,
a crisis of weather that never lets you arrive fully
at bitterness or sympathy.

My Parents' Grave

Inside the cemetery gate
my parents' grave has settled among the centuries.
In no time, my father will be a part of memory
for as long as he was a part of life.
There are other names commemorated here
to which they would both nod gently in recognition,
and on whose behalf, my mother would, no doubt,
add to the patina on Christ's feet
where they have been touched and kissed by legions.
My filial prayers summon their presence in the stone.
They say: you can't honour our memory
if you ridicule or dismiss our faith.
The stone stands constant against the breeze
that drifts between the crosses,
stirring the myriad colours of the leaves
and driving the eternal variations of the clouds.
I welcome their moral companionship
as I thoughtfully drift through their codes and cadences
back to the ferment outside the gate.

The Murky Universe

When you have no place in the world
the world itself is your place, but you can only breathe
its atmosphere of comfort from a distance.

I left the briery winter roads in a place purged of colour
where the future was soaked like a rag
in the murky lamp oil of the past.
That country was only vaguely in the world,
like everything hurt it lived in its memory.

But if you leave for long enough you leave forever,
the privilege to listen from within,
to kneel on the stony riverbed of communal prayer
and see with head down and eyes closed,
the same enormous God, the same murky universe.

Trail of Cold Smoke

Taking that trail of cold smoke
between loneliness and the burden of others,
I discovered that every distant light is a star
and every foreign sky a dome polished by prayer.

Confronted by the high walls of summer
I drank the yellow blood of desolate evenings
before wading into a tropical sleep that kept me weary.

In wintertime, I honed my voice
for small rooms and whispered prayers,
and played with the small sky of my breath on the frozen glass.

Though there was an air of accusation
in the way I regarded the world,
I loved the falling water of other people's voices
descending the cold steps of the urban night.

Nightfall

How immense and suffocating the world can be
as evening approaches: how the sway of a gentle requiem
overwhelms the earth.

Standing alone, I watch
a woman move through the street's remote affinities
carrying the cool perfume of the night to her corner of refuge.

To get through the twilight hours,
through the transition from marble to granite,
I need the bitter astringency of alcohol tasted in hunger.

Waiting

These vivid days without friendship or enmity
are a long white coastline along which I walk
waiting for word, I do not know from whom or from where.

There is no urgency,
though I keep my room ordered and my bag packed.
What is about to happen is fated.

Waiting is easy when I can hear the street
and see the sky from my bed.
I sleep with a calm fugitive spirit and the window open.

Sometimes I drink coffee among the suspect and forsaken
and listen to the sea's tender protest
as the night and the morning change ships.

Purity of Purpose

The air of this city
is prone to the boredom of poverty.
A grey sky sheds the light of exhumed bones on people's faces.

Infirm hands,
like birds locked out of their cages,
search without grace for things that are redeemable.

When it rains,
only the memory of a green country is aroused
but it is the yellow grass and the dusty hills that I am longing for.

I need to get back
to where the mountains and sky share the same altar of snow,
and to the vigorous rivers, cold and honest in their purity of purpose.

Pastoral Light

I come from the street to the leafy texture of this church
when I am homesick for devotion and pilgrimages in the rain.

I love the pastoral light, fragmented and softened through stained glass,
and how Egypt is evoked in the infinite distance
between the benches and the High Altar.

I love to watch solemn faces enacting a private ritual
and crabby old hands thumbing beads in a mosaic of shadows.

I love the young woman kneeling under the Sacred Heart,
the sweeping continent of her body, the rivers of light on her slender arms,
her closed eyes, her hidden breasts.

Grace

The vestibule is a frontier world,
its marble font a flower heavy after the rain.

The innate language of ritual pulls you in and down
to a tidal pool teeming with invisible life.

There is an aura of special and neglected things:
antique prayers – a flotilla of candles at the foot of a shrine.

Blessings and signs:
who would wish to live without such things—

and grace … that balancing act
that affords a commanding view.

Prayer

God, do not lose faith in me—
After all, it is your sky that keeps me wandering,
chained to my memories and premonitions.

God, do not loose faith in me—
After all, it is your ocean that keeps me homesick
for strange cities with antique hearts and indigenous music.

God, do not lose faith in me—
Sometimes I feel weary, and long for the depth of a single place—
one street, one door, with your house down the road.

Crisis of Faith

Night of closed flowers and extinguished candles
there is a door through which I see
rain falling on a column that houses a bell.

But all monuments are shadows
and the past is a ruin without walls
and it seems that life transpires without reason
and that exile breathes a fervent frost.

What is all this time swimming in our eyes
but the countenance of fire and an archive of old shoes.
Death is always present,
like the crest of a predatory animal drifting among the trees.

Fever

Because you had no plan, the summer dust,
potent with the shards of derelict cities,
oppressed you with overwhelming daydreams.

At night, you closed your eyes
and prayed for the refuge of sleep
believing that everything calm must be wise.

Returning on the summit of dawn
your candid lips opened with a vow of silence
and the resin of insatiable thirst.

Choosing a Colour

You can hear the sound of the poor
groping in the aisle of a tired Sunday
whose candles are longing to go out.

Mummified in the clothes of last December
their eyes are distant and gentle.
Luckily, they confide only their hunger,
as if their crises ended where yours begin.

Though the early stars goad their trail with yellow nails
they choose a colour from the twilight
in an appeal for comfort.

There is an air of premonition in their footsteps.
Their passions are deep, that is why they walk so slow
chasing a fugitive equilibrium
praising and lamenting a flawed creation.

Commotion in Paradise

The breeze stirs the leaves on the sidewalk.
Above the urban vortex of shadow and reflection
the eye of heaven dilates in the chromium sky.
Taken with an animal's dreamless hibernation,
its acceptance of sleep in order that the world can rest,
I am drawn away from the unremitting streets,
from tongues maddened with new languages,
to the incorruptible cadences of water—
the fluency of rivers and the choral wind.

Desolate Weather

Carrying the night like heavy water
from a sullen well,
every step I take is a ritual that moves
through desolate weather.

The spectral light of the city clock
is the breath of God
and the soft shadows of the deserted streets
are the agents of grief looking for prisoners.

Come back, I miss you.
The brave urban rain sings to your death
as I dwell on your life
under the faded green iron of the stars.

Succour

This moment of absence
and accumulated time
turns its blue light towards the river.

The fog officiates at a funeral ceremony
of footsteps and shadows.

You have left a wound on the world.
The mouths that you kissed are thirsty
while the moon passes it cup above their heads.

Family Feud

I hate the poor,
the way they walk so slow,
the way their dreams are visible
in a cage of glass.

I hate the way they touch each other
without intimacy.
I hate the way we wait, so tired
that heaven has no promise and hell no fear.

I hate the poor
the way the rich hate their families
because I know what they want,
I know what they're after.

Homework

With the damp monotony of a textbook,
the morning opened.
Down through the hours
he felt his spirit might succumb.

Now, in the early afternoon,
he pauses on the staircase,
preserved for generations
in a well of moribund light.

In a tall old window,
he sees the day hang like a backdrop
to a foolish school play,
tedious with lucent meaning,
futile as a wooden sword,

and he realizes there is more to life
than can be transcribed
and that his homework is to slay
whatever remains inside him of the day.

We Stayed So Late

We stayed so late
the furniture grew shadowy and deep

and the atmosphere shone with darkness
like polished brass.

We stayed so late
the room was skeletal without music

and we felt abandoned and sad
and happy to be together.

The world outside was empty
except of resignation for tomorrow.

The sky was dark and smooth
and blue as the future

and far away within us
a white wind swept over the past.

Reckoning

Because all you are
is a cup of water and a single star
the mockery of age continually asks
if it is still worth pursuing the world.

Acknowledging everything that is irrevocable,
a saffron sky offers you its opulent shelter
and walking there across the smoky medium of time
you assume the character of stone.

Evening in the Park

The paths are marked with flowers,
their cultivated fragrances
speak of funerals and sad marriages.

As dusk falls, a small pond
with the temperament of an indifferent lover
anchors a corner of the night under its dark stone.

The leaves of the trees
are abundant with enigmatic shadows,
deep with potent apprehension.

People walk here at dusk
because they love how the evening charms
more sadness from them than they believed they had.

Secluded Flower

In the adhesive gloom
its bright desolate gorge
sucks at the droning core
of shadow and light.
Fragile, ephemeral,
poised on a stem of green water,
patiently, meticulously,
it crosses the vast scintilla
of dawn, maturity and death.

The Bridge

Emerging from the condensation of stolen sleep
the morning carries its time from the river silently.
I awake and strike the damp match of my pain
but I refuse to feel homeless.

The bridge like a grey sunrise, sketched and bolted
on the world, is as a triumph of the spirit.
This mountain town stirs from sleep, its windows
deep and dark like the eyes of foreign women.

The river is as calm as wisdom.
The cold star of the first light reflected in the water
fills the shafts of the bridge's constant vigil,
asking for a first and final vow.

Borders

All the borders I have crossed
carrying the empty burden of my hunger
towards an horizon etched with secrets like a key.

All the borders I have crossed
while time softened my heart with summer storms
that un-scrolled in the sky dark roses of mystery and reckoning.

All the borders I have crossed
in reaching the cities my loneliness has given to me,
cities on fire with their own velocity.

The Onslaught of Emptiness

The festival is cast in fragments of colour and light.
Gravity has eased its hold, in a concert of birds,
bright fabrics and a sequence of revolving boats.

The disheveled air, dense with the odour
of seeds and candy, clings like sugar to the heavens.

There is a crude contagious happiness, pedestrian
as a souvenir, nurtured in an easy pattern of footsteps.

Wary of infectious happiness, I move to the edges of the festival
where the night approaches dressed as a nomadic woman,
drawn in by the fragrance of electricity and sand.

Brush Fire

The trees are bleeding in the shadows.
The sun is violent like a god of sand.
A small flame ignited by the air
eats the grass from tormented hands.

Though the herds of wild animals
maintain a serene countenance,
they raise their heads to the distance
in a rush of bewildered clairvoyance.

Almost Forgotten

The grace of the wilderness possesses the profile
of something important I had almost forgotten.

My hands have trembled often but they have never abdicated.
I have never become skilful at conjuring dreams without leaves or rain.

Only the veritable leaves and water can articulate
and the stones mitigate what my shadow needs to know.

I have become wiser and closer to home
when driven out by the force of my own misadventures

and when breathing the air around a kind woman's hair,
because desire is hope.

A Prairie Town

The sweet desolation of this small town
brings all the sensations of life to visit me.
Its storefronts wait for some commencement
and dreams that won't dissipate
linger within small houses that float outside history.

From the school, children's voices like scraps of paper
drift through the vast chamber
of the wayward afternoon.
I'm surprised to find the earth so tender.

I am drawn to the derelict railroad track
as one is drawn to a river. Old sheds,
perfumed with pitch and iron and neglect
are potent with the eyes of time.

The wind with its vow of poverty
blowing in from the yellow grass, deepens my life.
My attention moves from the whispering trees,
to the roofs of the town, to the neighbouring fields.

Abandoned Railroad Shed

The dust of confinement lay behind its bolted door,
a blend of industry gone idle
and departed souls shrouding their favoured stations.

This railroad shed has been locked for so long,
like a heart around its own slow season,
untouched by the revolving lathe of the world.

Saskatchewan Truck Stop

Through a waterfall of tempered glass
a world black as wet stone gathers around my cup.
A clock ticks like a leaf that fell yesterday.

Metallic wings of tired light, drawing their density from the night,
disturb the surfaces of old and unrequited memories:
They are the phantom guides that keep me restless.

Trusting and lost for so long behind impotent prayers,
with nothing being precise not even what I wish for,
the blue fuel of the night saturates my spirit.

Among the marooned cups and food consumed without communion,
masks of jaded brilliance, carved for ritual not flight,
participate indifferently in a liturgy of communal weariness.

Risen from clay, desolate as rain,
they look out from the shallow grave of loneliness
as the admonishing shoulders of God emerge on the horizon.

This Modest Hour

This modest hour is fitted to the world,
the stars perpetually lost
and the relentless motion of the sea
are complicit in this moment's grace.

I am exposed to the drama of your absence,
missing the light and warmth you carried off with you,
but I am happy in the broad expanse your absence gives me.

The tolling waves complain
that we can never leave the dead, that we are stuck with them,
and that the sea and its ropes are old
and tired of being fastened to this stone.

This Day is an Abdication

This day is an abdication—
the emptiness you delivered to me last night
won't let me open my door.

All my thoughts arrive
at pondering the road that you have taken,
at imagining the light that precedes and follows you.

The world didn't seem to need prayer
when you were with me
but now it wears a mantle of solicitation and rain.

Late One Saturday Night

The moon resting in her own shadow
floats above the harbour.

The ships with their painted names,
with their medallions and chains, are hollow and cold.

To be enamoured with emptiness and distances
is like loving a woman who doesn't care.

I am drunk and tired of my own heart,
tired of pursuing things that aren't there.

Stowaway

The sky is my only companion,
the sky I watched emerge at morning
above the line of your sleeping body,
a changeling woman who kept me lonely.

Unable to leave you,
I retreated into the ocean mist
that visits your balcony.

I am a stowaway on the ships you watch
leave the harbour at night
with passengers who voyage while sleeping.

Along the Waterfront

Along the waterfront
a transient light the colour of a hand
passes over a modest street,
lulled to sleep by complacent sadness.

The houses are husks in which un-harvested seeds
languish in the darkness of parched interiors.
On the street, a fine ocean mist like a runaway bride
pursues the transient light.

Low Tide

The fading day commiserates listlessly
like a tired mother.

Your heart is a boat at low tide
caught fast in the sand.

The ocean, fringed with rags and beads
rises and withdraws like a woman dancing.

The spiraling whale of the late evening sky
drifts on the firmament, distant and familiar.

The savage language of the wind and rain
lifts time from the world like greyness from a stone.

New Year

Snow falls on the sea.
Time passes, absorbed
into everything it touches.

Another year, smaller than the last,
is drawn out of the horizon
on cables of water and light.

After the Ritual

There is no repose in drunkenness: its prize is an odyssey
through fractured light, the keening rain and other people's comfort.

That impetuous world, turning on a coil of poisoned blood,
pulls the heavens close and magnifies the sudden shower of my life,
but it is framed by death's immutable light.

After the ritual, I sleep between the horns of the altar
dressed in the thick smoke of extinguished candles.

When I wake again, to the verdant flower of addiction,
the radio sounds like a star in crisis
as the stone angel of the day fades towards visibility.

Ghost Story

Old town, I have a ghost who lives here,
when will you let me roll back the soft stone of the sky
and let my ghost escape.

The fragrance of an eternally long dispossessed evening
always emanates from your coat of wet snow.
Your abiding heart of deep water is always awake, always watching,

and although you are as kind as Jesus,
sometimes I'm afraid that I will find neither refuge nor repose
among your crosses of sloping streets.

Old town, when can I throw off the soft stone of the sky
that weighs on me like empathy that has been endured for too long.
Grey templed old town: let my ghost escape, let me take his place.

The Sea at Night

From the beach that night,
the sea was tall and ominous
frightening and magnificent
like sleep to a child.

With every parade of the waves,
a line of marching drummers disappeared.
The nomadic appendages of the clouds
floated over the thin soup of the moon
and the world turned out towards heaven
and in towards itself, like the vortex of a shell.

Because the tendency of water is to leave,
the sea that night pulled us closer to each other,
allowing us to feel forsaken together,
happy and in accord.